This Book Belongs To:

_____

COPYRIGHT © 2004 Nanci Bell
Gander Publishing
P.O. Box 780, 450 Front Street
Avila Beach, CA 93424
805-541-5523 • 800-554-1819

VISUALIZING AND VERBALIZING AND V/V ARE REGISTERED TRADEMARKS OF NANCI BELL.

All rights reserved. No part of this material shall be reproduced or transmitted in any form or by any means, electronic or mechanical, including photocopying, recording, or by any information or retrieval system, without prior written permission from the Publisher. Production and design were directed by Valarie Jones. Contributing writers and editors were Ben Earl, Valarie Jones, Katelyn Mirolla, Ariana Spaulding, and Michael Sweeney. Printed in the U.S.A.

17 16 15 14   4 5 6 7

ISBN 0-945856-46-6   978-0-945856-46-7

Overview and Directions

This workbook is designed to develop gestalt imagery and language comprehension with the *Visualizing and Verbalizing for Language Comprehension and Thinking*® (V/V®) program.

Following the steps of V/V, detail and gestalt imagery are developed with Sentence by Sentence, Multiple Sentence, Whole Paragraph, and Paragraph by Paragraph V/V stimulation.

Each story is high in imagery and followed by these workbook activities:

- Imagery Questions
- Picture Summary
- Word Summary
- Main Idea
- Higher Order Thinking (HOT) Questions
- Paragraph Writing

As the student begins each story, he/she should decode the vocabulary words and visualize the meaning. This will help create imagery and develop contextual fluency. The student may write phrases or partial sentences to describe his/her imagery.

These workbooks have been written specifically to help students learn and discover the wonder of the written word by improving gestalt imagery, critical thinking, and writing skills. Once these skills are developed, the possibilities are endless.

Remember, you can help students do this. You can do anything!

Nanci Bell
2004

There are three workbooks at each reading level:

Book A • Sentence by Sentence
Book B • Sentence by Sentence and Multiple Sentence
Book C • Multiple Sentence, Whole Paragraph, and Paragraph by Paragraph

1 Honey Harvest

A small man started a fire on the jungle floor after clearing an area of leaves. Above his head on a tree hung a beehive, with a few bees buzzing around it calmly. / He threw lots of leaves on the fire to create thick gray smoke. He didn't run away when a cloud of buzzing bees suddenly swarmed madly around him. / He took his mud-coated arm and thrust it into the brown hive. He tore out a chunk of sticky golden honeycomb. / He ignored many painful stings as he gobbled the gooey treat. Then he pulled out more and placed it in a woven basket.

Vocabulary to Visualize:

beehive: a home for bees
swarmed: a large number of insects flying together
thrust: pushed
honeycomb: a group of wax cells that bees store honey in
gobbled: ate quickly

---

1 **First and Second Sentences:** A small man started a fire on the jungle floor after clearing an area of leaves. Above his head on a tree hung a beehive, with a few bees buzzing around it calmly.

What did those words make you picture? _____

What did you picture for...

1. the man? _____

2. the area he cleared of leaves? _____

3. the fire? _____

4. the beehive? _____

---

2 **Third and Fourth Sentences:** He threw lots of leaves on the fire to create thick gray smoke. He didn't run away when a cloud of buzzing bees suddenly swarmed madly around him.

What did those words make you picture? _____

What did you picture for...

1. the man throwing leaves? _____

2. the smoke? _____

3. the swarm of bees? _____

4. the sound of their buzzing? _____

3 **Fifth and Sixth Sentences:** He took his mud-coated arm and thrust it into the brown hive. He tore out a chunk of sticky golden honeycomb.

What did those words make you picture? _____
_____
_____

What did you picture for...

1. the man's arm? _____

2. him thrusting it into the hive? _____

3. the chunk of honeycomb? _____

4. him tearing the chunk out? _____

4 **Seventh and Eighth Sentences:** He ignored many painful stings as he gobbled the gooey treat. Then he pulled out more and placed it in a woven basket.

What did those words make you picture? _____
_____
_____

What did you picture for...

1. the stings? _____

2. the gooey treat? _____

3. him gobbling the treat? _____

4. the basket? _____

Picture Summary:

Number your images in order.

☐ The man pulled out honeycomb and placed it in a basket.

☐ The man started a fire under a beehive hanging in a tree.

☐ The man shoved his mud-coated hand into the beehive, ignoring the buzzing bees.

☐ The man pulled out a chunk of honeycomb and ate it.

Write a Word Summary:

_____
_____
_____
_____
_____
_____
_____
_____

Critical Thinking

Main Idea:

Check the box that best describes all your images—the main idea.

☐ A small man made a fire under a beehive and grabbed some honeycomb out of the hive while the bees swarmed around him.

☐ A man wearing only leaves and grass started a fire under a tree, piling on leaves to create a thick gray smoke.

☐ The gray smoke sent the bees out swarming and angry, and the man ignored their many painful stings.

HOT Questions:

1. Why do you think the man started a fire on the jungle floor? _____

2. Why do you think the fire was under a beehive? _____

3. Why do you think the man threw leaves on the fire? _____

4. Why might a smoky fire be important to the man? _____

5. Why do you think he covered his arm in mud? _____

6. What do you think the smoke did to the bees? _____

7. Why do you think the man put some honeycomb into a basket? _____

Write a Story

Make up a story about what might have happened if you tried to get honey out of a beehive.

Did you use all of the Structure Words? Check each one you used.
- ☐ What
- ☐ Number
- ☐ Color
- ☐ Mood
- ☐ Background
- ☐ Perspective
- ☐ Size
- ☐ Shape
- ☐ Movement
- ☐ Where
- ☐ When
- ☐ Sound

2 The Volcano

Mount Saint Helens was a snowy dormant volcano that the American Indians used to call "Fire Mountain." In 1980, the tall mountain began to rumble and blow steam from its top. / Excited news crews from all over the world brought cameras to record it. Scientists studied a bulge on one side of the mountain that grew bigger each day. / The volcano growled and smoked for two months until a large earthquake shook it one morning. Smoke, ash, and lava exploded out from the bulge. / The force of the blast flattened the forest for miles. Dark clouds of ash covered cities hundreds of miles away and made day seem as dark as night.

Vocabulary to Visualize:

Mount St. Helens: a volcano in the state of Washington
dormant: not active; still
American Indians: the first peoples to live in North America
bulge: a swollen area

---

1 **First and Second Sentences:** Mount Saint Helens was a snowy dormant volcano that the American Indians used to call "Fire Mountain." In 1980, the tall mountain began to rumble and blow steam from its top.

What did those words make you picture? _____

_____

What did you picture for...

1. Mount Saint Helens? _____

2. a "dormant" volcano? _____

3. the mountain rumbling? _____

4. it blowing steam? _____

2 **Third and Fourth Sentences:** Excited news crews from all over the world brought cameras to record it. Scientists studied a bulge on one side of the mountain that grew bigger each day.

What did those words make you picture? _____

_____

What did you picture for...

1. news crews recording it? _____

2. scientists studying it? _____

3. the bulge on one side? _____

4. the bulge growing? _____

3 **Fifth and Sixth Sentences:** The volcano growled and smoked for two months until a large earthquake shook it one morning. Smoke, ash, and lava exploded out from the bulge.
   What did those words make you picture? _____
   _____
   _____

What did you picture for...

1. the sound of the volcano growling? _____
   _____

2. the volcano smoking? _____
   _____

3. the earthquake shaking it? _____
   _____

4. the explosion? _____
   _____

4 **Seventh and Eighth Sentences:** The force of the blast flattened the forest for miles. Dark clouds of ash covered cities hundreds of miles away and made day seem as dark as night.
   What did those words make you picture? _____
   _____
   _____

What did you picture for...

1. the blast? _____
   _____

2. the forests being flattened? _____
   _____

3. the dark clouds of ash? _____
   _____

4. day seeming like night? _____
   _____

Picture Summary:

Number your images in order.

- Scientists and news crews studied the bulge growing on one side of the volcano and recorded its smoking and rumbling.

- Mount Saint Helens, a volcano known as "Fire Mountain," lay dormant and covered with snow.

- An earthquake shook the volcano and a huge blast shot out lava, ash, and smoke.

- Ash filled the skies for hundreds of miles, making them as dark as night.

Write a Word Summary:

_____
_____
_____
_____
_____
_____
_____
_____

Critical Thinking

Main Idea:

Check the box that best describes all your images—the main idea.

☐ Mt. Saint Helens was a cone-shaped volcano mountain that was called "Fire Mountain" by the American Indians.

☐ As the world watched, Mt. Saint Helens rumbled and bulged before finally exploding outward, sending ash and lava into the sky.

☐ Mt. Saint Helens smoked and rumbled, watched by scientists and news crews for days, before it went back to being dormant.

HOT Questions:

1. Why do you think the American Indians called Mt. Saint Helens "Fire Mountain"? _____

2. Why do you think the side of the mountain was bulging? _____

3. Why do you think the news crews were excited? _____

4. Why do you think the scientists wanted to study it? _____

5. How might the earthquake be connected to the volcano's eruption? _____

6. Do you think the explosion was powerful? Why or why not? _____

7. Why do you think the day seemed like night even far away? _____

Write a Story

Make up a story about a scientist watching Mt. Saint Helens when it erupts.

Did you use all of the Structure Words? Check each one you used.

- ☐ What
- ☐ Number
- ☐ Color
- ☐ Mood
- ☐ Background
- ☐ Perspective
- ☐ Size
- ☐ Shape
- ☐ Movement
- ☐ Where
- ☐ When
- ☐ Sound

3 Cashmere

Cashmere wool, called the Cloth of Kings, is made from the fur of a longhaired goat. The goat has two spiraled horns and a thick white coat. / His coat has two layers of fur, a soft fine down and a coarse outer layer called guard hair. The goat is sheared and the fleece is dehaired to remove the guard hair from the softer fur. / The silky fur is then washed, dyed, and spun into yarn. The cashmere yarn is made into luxurious garments such as coats, scarves, skirts, and sweaters. / These fine clothes are very soft, long lasting, and extra warm during cold times of the year. The cashmere is highly prized by royalty and other rich folk.

Vocabulary to Visualize:

cashmere: wool from a type of goat found in Kashmir and Tibet
spiraled: curves in a circular way, like a screw
down: small soft fur or feathers
sheared: shaved or cut off
fleece: the wool of an animal
luxurious: expensive and fine
prized: given high value; wanted very badly

1 **First and Second Sentences:** Cashmere wool, called the Cloth of Kings, is made from the fur of a longhaired goat. The goat has two spiraled horns and a thick white coat.

What did those words make you picture? _____

What did you picture for...

1. the goat? _____

2. his horns? _____

3. his white coat? _____

4. cashmere? _____

2 **Third and Fourth Sentences:** His coat has two layers of fur, a soft fine down and a coarse outer layer called guard hair. The goat is sheared and the fleece is dehaired to remove the guard hair from the softer fur.

What did those words make you picture? _____

What did you picture for...

1. two layers of fur? _____

2. the guard hair? _____

3. the goat being sheared? _____

4. the fleece being dehaired? _____

3 **Fifth and Sixth Sentences:** The silky fur is then washed, dyed, and spun into yarn. The cashmere yarn is made into luxurious garments such as coats, scarves, skirts, and sweaters.
What did those words make you picture? _____
_____
_____

What did you picture for...

1. the silky fur? _____
_____

2. the fur being washed? _____
_____

3. the fur being dyed? _____
_____

4. the coats and scarves? _____
_____

4 **Seventh and Eighth Sentences:** These fine clothes are very soft, long lasting, and extra warm during cold times of the year. The cashmere is highly prized by royalty and other rich folk.
What did those words make you picture? _____
_____
_____

What did you picture for...

1. fine clothes? _____
_____

2. the clothes being extra warm? _____
_____

3. cashmere being highly prized? _____
_____

4. royalty? _____
_____

Picture Summary:

Number your images in order.

☐ The goat is sheared and the fleece is dehaired.

☐ The goat has an outer layer of coarse hair and an inner layer of soft down.

☐ Cashmere wool is highly prized by royalty and rich people.

☐ The cashmere yarn is spun into fine sweaters and scarves.

Write a Word Summary:

_____
_____
_____
_____
_____
_____
_____
_____

Critical Thinking

Main Idea:

Check the box that best describes all your images—the main idea.

☐ The cashmere goat is longhaired, with both a coarse coat of long outer hair and an inner coat of soft down, as well as spiraled horns.

☐ Cashmere, taken from the coat of a goat and made into fine clothing, is prized by the rich for its softness and warmth.

☐ Once a goat is sheared, the fleece is dehaired to remove the soft down from the coarse outer fur.

HOT Questions:

1. Why do you think cashmere wool is called the Cloth of Kings? _____

2. Why do you think the goat is sheared? _____

3. Why do you think the coarse hair needs to be removed from the silky fur? _____

4. Why do you think the silky fur is washed and dyed? _____

5. Why do you think the fur is spun? _____

6. Why do you think the cashmere yarn is made into garments? _____

7. Why do you think cashmere is highly prized by royalty and rich folk? _____

Write a Story

Make up an exciting story about someone catching a goat high in the mountains.

_____
_____
_____
_____
_____
_____
_____
_____
_____
_____
_____
_____
_____
_____
_____
_____
_____
_____
_____

Did you use all of the Structure Words? Check each one you used.

☐ What	☐ Number	☐ Color	☐ Mood	☐ Background	☐ Perspective
☐ Size	☐ Shape	☐ Movement	☐ Where	☐ When	☐ Sound

4 The Trojan War

A huge Greek army set out to invade Troy, a great city protected by high walls of stone. A fleet of 1,000 Greek ships landed on the beaches near Troy ready for war. / The Greeks fought outside the city for ten years, but they could not break the strong walls of Troy. So the Greeks built a large wooden horse and hid a few soldiers inside. / It was left in front of the city walls while the Greek army pretended to retreat. Once the enemy was gone, the Trojans lugged the heavy gift horse inside their walls. / During the night, the Greek soldiers snuck out of the horse and opened the huge city gates to let their army, who was hiding nearby, in. They burned the city down.

Vocabulary to Visualize:

Trojan: of or from Troy
Greek: in or from Greece, a country in Southern Europe
Troy: an ancient city in Asia
fleet: a large group of ships
retreat: surrender and leave
lugged: carried with effort

---

1. First and Second Sentences: A huge Greek army set out to invade Troy, a great city protected by high walls of stone. A fleet of 1,000 Greek ships landed on the beaches near Troy ready for war.

What did those words make you picture? _____

What did you picture for...

1. the Greek army? _____

2. Troy? _____

3. the city walls? _____

4. the ships? _____

---

2. Third and Fourth Sentences: The Greeks fought outside the city for ten years, but they could not break the strong walls of Troy. So the Greeks built a large wooden horse and hid a few soldiers inside.

What did those words make you picture? _____

What did you picture for...

1. the fighting? _____

2. ten years passing? _____

3. the wooden horse? _____

4. the soldiers inside? _____

3 **Fifth and Sixth Sentences:** It was left in front of the city walls while the Greek army pretended to retreat. Once the enemy was gone, the Trojans lugged the heavy gift horse inside their walls.
What did those words make you picture? _____
_____
_____

What did you picture for...

1. the horse being left? _____
_____

2. the Greek army retreating? _____
_____

3. the Trojans lugging the horse? _____
_____

4. the horse inside of their walls? _____
_____

4 **Seventh and Eighth Sentences:** During the night, the Greek soldiers snuck out of the horse and opened the huge city gates to let their army, who was hiding nearby, in. They burned the city down.
What did those words make you picture? _____
_____
_____

What did you picture for...

1. the soldiers sneaking out? _____
_____

2. them opening the city gates? _____
_____

3. the army coming in? _____
_____

4. the city burning down? _____
_____

Picture Summary:

Number your images in order.

☐ The Trojans dragged the big wooden horse inside their city walls.

☐ The Greek soldiers inside the horse opened the gates and the Greeks burned the city.

☐ The Greek army fought outside the strong walls of Troy for ten years.

☐ The Greeks built a large wooden horse and hid a few soldiers inside of it.

Write a Word Summary:

_____
_____
_____
_____
_____
_____
_____
_____
_____
_____

Critical Thinking

Main Idea:

Check the box that best describes all your images—the main idea.

☐ The Trojans had high city walls that the Greek army could not break in ten years of fighting, so the Greek army left.

☐ After ten years of fighting outside the walls of Troy, the Greek army built a horse to sneak soldiers into the city gates.

☐ The Greek army landed at Troy with 1,000 ships and a huge Greek army, but they couldn't break the walls of the great city.

HOT Questions:

1. Why do you think so many ships sailed to Troy? _____

2. Why do you think the walls of stone helped protect Troy? _____

3. Why do you think they were still fighting after ten years? _____

4. Why do you think the Greeks built a wooden horse? _____

5. Why do you think Greek soldiers hid inside the horse? _____

6. Why do you think the Trojans lugged the horse inside their walls? _____

7. Why do you think the hidden soldiers opened the city gates at night? _____

Write a Story

Make up an adventurous tale about being one of the soldiers inside the wooden horse.

Did you use all of the Structure Words? Check each one you used.

- ☐ What
- ☐ Number
- ☐ Color
- ☐ Mood
- ☐ Background
- ☐ Perspective
- ☐ Size
- ☐ Shape
- ☐ Movement
- ☐ Where
- ☐ When
- ☐ Sound

5 California Condor

It was a sad day when the last wild condor was caught and taken to the zoo. It took three men to hold the large black bird with strong wings down, and get it into the cage. / Once, thousands of condors, with wingspans almost ten feet across, soared high in the skies. Most were killed by hunters or from eating trash like bottle caps and plastic bags. / The last twenty-seven condors were caught and taken to live in zoos, where they would be safe. Their eggs and chicks were taken care of by zookeepers. / In ten years, there were enough condors to release some back into the wild. Once they are tagged with numbers on their wings, they are taken far from the city and freed.

Vocabulary to Visualize:

California: a state on the western side of the United States
condor: a large vulture
tagged: marked for identification

1
First and Second Sentences: It was a sad day when the last wild condor was caught and taken to the zoo. It took three men to hold the large black bird with strong wings down, and get it into the cage.

What did those words make you picture? _____

_____

_____

What did you picture for...

1. the condor? _____

_____

2. the condor being caught? _____

_____

3. the cage? _____

_____

4. the zoo? _____

2
Third and Fourth Sentences: Once, thousands of condors, with wingspans almost ten feet across, soared high in the skies. Most were killed by hunters or from eating trash like bottle caps and plastic bags.

What did those words make you picture? _____

_____

_____

What did you picture for...

1. thousands of condors? _____

_____

2. the wingspan of a condor? _____

_____

3. condors being hunted? _____

_____

4. bottle caps? _____

3 **Fifth and Sixth Sentences:** The last twenty-seven condors were caught and taken to live in zoos, where they would be safe. Their eggs and chicks were taken care of by zookeepers.
What did those words make you picture? _____
_____
_____

What did you picture for...

1. the zoos? _____
   _____

2. the condors living in zoos? _____
   _____

3. their eggs? _____
   _____

4. their chicks? _____
   _____

4 **Seventh and Eighth Sentences:** In ten years, there were enough condors to release some back into the wild. Once they are tagged with numbers on their wings, they are taken far from the city and freed.
What did those words make you picture? _____
_____
_____

What did you picture for...

1. the numbered tag? _____
   _____

2. tagging a condor? _____
   _____

3. condors being taken far from the city? _____
   _____

4. condors being freed? _____
   _____

Picture Summary:
Number your images in order.

   The condors live at zoos, where zookeepers take care of their eggs and chicks.

   The last wild condor was caught and put in a cage by three men.

   There were only twenty-seven wild condors left when they were all caught and taken to zoos.

   In ten years, there were enough condors to release some back into the wild after tagging.

Write a Word Summary:

_____
_____
_____
_____
_____
_____
_____

Critical Thinking

Main Idea:

Check the box that best describes all your images—the main idea.

☐ Thousands of wild condors soar in the skies over the cities and zoos.

☐ Only twenty-seven condors were left when they were caught and taken to the zoo to be saved.

☐ It took three men to hold a big condor down and get it inside a cage.

HOT Questions:

1. Why do you think the last condor had to be caught? _____

2. Why do you think it took three men to hold the condor? _____

3. Why do you think there were only twenty-seven wild condors left? _____

4. Why do you think the condors went from thousands to only twenty-seven in the wild? _____

5. Why do you think all twenty-seven wild condors were taken to zoos? _____

6. Do you think it is important that zookeepers took care of the eggs and chicks? Why or why not? _____

7. Why do you think the condors are released far from the city? _____

Write a Story

Make up a story about a condor being caught and living in the zoo.

_____

Did you use all of the Structure Words? Check each one you used.
- ☐ What
- ☐ Size
- ☐ Number
- ☐ Shape
- ☐ Color
- ☐ Movement
- ☐ Mood
- ☐ Where
- ☐ Background
- ☐ When
- ☐ Perspective
- ☐ Sound

6 La Quinceañera

La Quinceañera is a Latino rite of passage that celebrates a girl turning fifteen. It is an all-day event to honor her leaving childhood and becoming a woman. / The day starts with her joining her happy relatives at a church service held just for her. She dresses in a formal white gown and wears a tiara on her head. / Then, holding flowers, she kneels on a pillow that has her name on it at the church altar. She chooses some friends to be her *damas* and *chambelanes* during the special mass. / After the service, she is met by friends and family at a fancy reception. The party includes live music, food, and dancing all night long.

Vocabulary to Visualize:

Latino: of Spanish-speaking or Latin-American descent
rite of passage: an important act that marks the move from one stage of life to another
service: religious meeting; mass
tiara: a half crown worn on the head
altar: a table or structure where religious rites are performed
damas: Spanish for ladies
chambelanes: Spanish for gentlemen

---

1. First and Second Sentences: La Quinceañera is a Latino rite of passage that celebrates a girl turning fifteen. It is an all-day event to honor her leaving childhood and becoming a woman.

What did those words make you picture? _____

What did you picture for...

1. a rite of passage? _____

2. a fifteen-year old girl? _____

3. an all-day event? _____

4. leaving childhood? _____

---

2. Third and Fourth Sentences: The day starts with her joining her happy relatives at a church service held just for her. She dresses in a formal white gown and wears a tiara on her head.

What did those words make you picture? _____

What did you picture for...

1. her relatives? _____

2. the church service? _____

3. her gown? _____

4. her tiara? _____

3 **Fifth and Sixth Sentences:** Then, holding flowers, she kneels on a pillow that has her name on it at the church altar. She chooses some friends to be her *damas* and *chambelanes* during the special mass.
What did those words make you picture? _____
_____
_____

What did you picture for...

1. the flowers? _____
   _____

2. her kneeling? _____
   _____

3. the pillow? _____
   _____

4. her damas and chambelanes? _____
   _____

4 **Seventh and Eighth Sentences:** After the service, she is met by friends and family at a fancy reception. The party includes live music, food, and dancing all night long.
What did those words make you picture? _____
_____
_____

What did you picture for...

1. her friends and family? _____
   _____

2. the reception? _____
   _____

3. live music? _____
   _____

4. dancing all night long? _____
   _____

Picture Summary:

Number your images in order.

☐ For La Quinceañera, the girl chooses friends, her damas and chambelanes.

☐ La Quinceañera includes a special mass where the girl wears a white gown and tiara.

☐ La Quinceañera is the celebration of a girl turning fifteen in Latino culture.

☐ La Quinceañera includes a fancy reception with live music and dancing all night.

Write a Word Summary:

_____
_____
_____
_____
_____
_____
_____
_____

Critical Thinking

Main Idea:

Check the box that best describes all your images—the main idea.

☐ In Latino culture, La Quinceañera is a special mass followed by a festive party celebrating a girl becoming a woman.

☐ La Quinceañera is a Latino rite of passage that includes a special mass where the girl wears a white gown and a tiara to church.

☐ La Quinceañera is a time when a girl leaves childhood behind and picks certain friends to be her damas and chambelanes.

HOT Questions:

1. Why do you think there is a big celebration when a Latina girl turns fifteen? _____

2. Why do you think La Quinceañera might be an all-day event? _____

3. Why do you think she dresses in a formal white gown? _____

4. Why do you think her close relatives join her at the church service? _____

5. Why do you think turning fifteen is a special time? _____

6. Why do you think there is a fancy reception following the ceremony? _____

7. Do you think the birthday girl danced at the reception? Why or why not? _____

Write a Story

Make up a story about something funny happening at a Quinceañera party.

___

Did you use all of the Structure Words? Check each one you used.
- ☐ What
- ☐ Number
- ☐ Color
- ☐ Mood
- ☐ Background
- ☐ Perspective
- ☐ Size
- ☐ Shape
- ☐ Movement
- ☐ Where
- ☐ When
- ☐ Sound

7 The Molimo

The Mbuti men sit around the *kumamolimo* for the molimo festival. The firewood collected by young men from each hut in the tribe burns bright. / With the women and children safe in their huts, the men start to sing and chant. Suddenly, the fabled but never seen molimo calls out from the jungle. / Then the men answer and wait for the beast to whistle or growl back. They sing for hours about the food gathered to honor him, until the molimo has been silent for a while. / Then the tribe's best singer sneaks out of the jungle to join the men as they hurry to eat the food. The women quake as they hear the molimo eat, but the men know the truth.

Vocabulary to Visualize:

molimo: an imaginary scary creature from Mbuti myth
Mbuti: (*em-boo-tee*) a tribe of people living in the Ituri rainforest in the Congo, a country in Africa
kumamolimo: a special bonfire
fabled: from myth or legend

---

1 **First and Second Sentences:** The Mbuti men sit around the *kumamolimo* for the molimo festival. The firewood collected by young men from each hut in the tribe burns bright.

What did those words make you picture? _____

What did you picture for...

1. the kumamolimo? _____

2. the Mbuti men around the fire? _____

3. firewood collected by young men? _____

4. the festival? _____

---

2 **Third and Fourth Sentences:** With the women and children safe in their huts, the men start to sing and chant. Suddenly, the fabled but never seen molimo calls out from the jungle.

What did those words make you picture? _____

What did you picture for...

1. the women and children in their huts? _____

2. the men singing and chanting? _____

3. the fabled molimo? _____

4. it calling out from the jungle? _____

3
Fifth and Sixth Sentences: Then the men answer and wait for the molimo to whistle or growl back. They sing for hours about the food gathered to honor him, until the molimo has been silent for a while.

What did those words make you picture? _____
_____
_____

What did you picture for...

1. the men's answer? _____

2. the molimo's growl? _____

3. the food gathered? _____

4. the men singing for hours? _____

4
Seventh and Eighth Sentences: Then the tribe's best singer sneaks out of the jungle to join the men as they hurry to eat the food. The women quake as they hear the molimo eat, but the men know the truth.

What did those words make you picture? _____
_____
_____

What did you picture for...

1. the tribe's best singer? _____

2. him sneaking out of the jungle? _____

3. the women quaking? _____

4. the mood of the men? _____

Picture Summary:

Number your images in order.

☐ The men sing and chant around the kumamolimo while the women and children hide in their huts.

☐ The molimo growls and whistles at the men, and they all sing for hours.

☐ The molimo and the men eat the food gathered to honor the molimo.

☐ The tribe's best singer sneaks out of the forest to join the men eating food.

Write a Word Summary:

_____
_____
_____
_____
_____
_____
_____
_____
_____
_____

Critical Thinking

Main Idea:

Check the box that best describes all your images—the main idea.

☐ In the molimo festival of the Mbuti tribe the men and women sing around a fire while the unseen molimo answers from the forest.

☐ The Mbuti men build a great fire called a kumamolimo and sit around it singing all through the night.

☐ During the Mbuti festival that honors the molimo, the women hide and the men sing and eat food.

HOT Questions:

1. Why might the men build a great fire? _____

2. Why might they have to collect firewood from each hut? _____

3. Why do you think the women and children stay inside their huts? _____

4. Why do you think the men sing and chant? _____

5. Why might the Mbuti have gathered the food? _____

6. Do you think the molimo is real? Why or why not? _____

7. What might be the purpose of the molimo festival? _____

Write a Story

Make up a scary story about the tribe's best singer as he goes into the jungle one night during the festival.

Did you use all of the Structure Words? Check each one you used.
- ☐ What
- ☐ Number
- ☐ Color
- ☐ Mood
- ☐ Background
- ☐ Perspective
- ☐ Size
- ☐ Shape
- ☐ Movement
- ☐ Where
- ☐ When
- ☐ Sound

8 Winchester Mystery House

The Winchester Mystery House in San Jose is a large mansion with a red roof and 160 rooms. Building on the house began in 1884 by Sarah Winchester, the heiress to a fortune. / She thought ghosts of those who had been killed by the rifle her now-dead husband invented haunted her. She thought that as long as she kept building, the spirits would not harm her. / For thirty-eight years, Sarah kept men at work all day and night pounding nails and sawing wood. Room after room was put up to fool and mislead the spirits. / Staircases led nowhere, doors opened into walls, and windows were built in the floor. Today, people can tour the house's maze of rooms.

Vocabulary to Visualize:

San Jose: a city in Northern California
mansion: a large and grand house
heiress: a woman due to inherit
rifle: a type of gun with a long barrel
invented: made for the first time
mislead: confuse or deceive
maze: a system of passages designed to confuse

---

1 **First and Second Sentences:** The Winchester Mystery House in San Jose is a large mansion with a red roof and 160 rooms. Building on the house began in 1884 by Sarah Winchester, the heiress to a fortune.

What did those words make you picture? _____

What did you picture for...

1. the house? _____

2. the roof? _____

3. the rooms in the mansion? _____

4. Sarah Winchester? _____

---

2 **Third and Fourth Sentences:** She thought ghosts of those who had been killed by the rifle her now-dead husband invented haunted her. She thought that as long as she kept building, the spirits would not harm her.

What did those words make you picture? _____

What did you picture for...

1. ghosts? _____

2. them haunting her? _____

3. building on her house? _____

4. Sarah's mood? _____

3 **Fifth and Sixth Sentences:** For thirty-eight years, Sarah kept men at work all day and night pounding nails and sawing wood. Room after room was put up to fool and mislead the spirits.
What did those words make you picture? _____
_____
_____

What did you picture for...

1. thirty-eight years? _____
_____

2. the men at work? _____
_____

3. men pounding nails? _____
_____

4. the spirits being fooled? _____
_____

4 **Seventh and Eighth Sentences:** Staircases led nowhere, doors opened into walls, and windows were built in the floor. Today, people can tour the house's maze of rooms.
What did those words make you picture? _____
_____
_____

What did you picture for...

1. the staircases? _____
_____

2. doors opening into walls? _____
_____

3. windows in the floor? _____
_____

4. a maze of rooms? _____
_____

Picture Summary:

Number your images in order.

☐ The men added staircases that led nowhere and windows in the floor in the maze of rooms.

☐ Sarah believed that the ghosts of people killed by the gun her husband invented haunted her.

☐ Sarah kept men building for thirty-eight years non-stop so that the ghosts would not harm her.

☐ People come to visit the house and see the maze of rooms.

Write a Word Summary:

_____
_____
_____
_____
_____
_____
_____
_____

Critical Thinking

Main Idea:

Check the box that best describes all your images—the main idea.

☐ Sarah Winchester kept men at work for thirty-eight years building rooms onto the Winchester Mystery House.

☐ The Winchester Mystery House was built over thirty-eight years into a maze by Sarah Winchester to keep away ghosts.

☐ The Winchester Mystery House has a maze of rooms, windows in the floor, and staircases leading nowhere that people can visit.

HOT Questions:

1. Why do you think Sarah Winchester thought she was haunted? _____

2. Do you think Sarah would have still built the mansion if she hadn't inherited a fortune? Why or why not? _____

3. Why do you think she hired workers instead of building the rooms herself? _____

4. Why do you think the mansion had doors that opened into walls? _____

5. Why do you think Sarah might have wanted to fool the spirits? _____

6. Why do you think the Winchester mansion is considered mysterious? _____

7. Why might people want to visit the mansion? _____

Write a Story

Make up a spooky story about the Winchester Mystery House on Halloween night.

Did you use all of the Structure Words? Check each one you used.
- ☐ What
- ☐ Size
- ☐ Number
- ☐ Shape
- ☐ Color
- ☐ Movement
- ☐ Mood
- ☐ Where
- ☐ Background
- ☐ When
- ☐ Perspective
- ☐ Sound

9 The African *Griot*

The African tribe gathers around the fire at night to listen to the griot tell stories. The revered griot stands up in front of the entire tribe and begins to speak. During the story, he waves his hands around in the air and his voice switches from loud to soft. He enthralls his audience as he makes the story come alive. He speaks of their ancestors and their way of life, and reminds the tribe of how they came to be. It is the duty of the griot to carry on the oral history of his tribe.

Whole Paragraph
Date: _____

Vocabulary to Visualize:

African: of or from Africa, a continent that is south of Europe
griot: an African storyteller
revered: held in high regard; respected
enthralls: captivates; interests greatly
ancestors: relatives from whom a person is descended
oral: spoken, not written

1 What did those words make you picture? _____

What did you picture for...

1. the African tribe? _____

2. them gathering around the fire? _____

3. the griot? _____

4. his hands? _____

5. his voice? _____

Critical Thinking

Write a Word Summary:

_____

_____

_____

_____

_____

Main Idea:

Check the box that best describes all your images—the main idea.

☐ The African tribe gathers at night to hear stories from the griot about the history of the tribe.

☐ The African griot waves his hands and lowers and raises his voice as he tells stories.

☐ The African tribe gathers the griots to hear stories about the tribe's history at night.

HOT Questions:

1. Why do you think the tribe gathers around the fire at night? _____

_____

2. Why do you think the griot uses his hands while telling stories? _____

_____

3. Why do you think his voice switches from loud to soft while telling stories? _____

_____

4. Why do you think the audience is enthralled? _____

_____

5. Do you think it might be important for the griot to share the tribe's history? Why or why not? _____

_____

6. How do you think the griot learned the tribe's history? _____

_____

10 The Camel

The large brown camel can survive for long periods of time in the hot and dry desert without much food or water. He is seven feet tall and has two firm humps on his back that store fat. This fat is used for food to give the camel energy when he has nothing to eat. When he is starving, the humps will shrink in size. The humps may become limp and droop over on the side of his body. But when he is given time to rest and eat, his humps will become hard again and stick back up on his back.

Vocabulary to Visualize:

periods: amounts of time
desert: a dry and sandy area with little water and few plants or animals
firm: solid to the touch
store: put away; keep for later use
limp: not firm; lacking stiffness
droop: sag, hang down, or bend

Whole Paragraph
Date: _____

1 What did those words make you picture? _____

What did you picture for...

1. the camel? _____

2. the desert? _____

3. his humps shrinking in size? _____

4. his humps drooping over? _____

5. his humps becoming hard again? _____

Critical Thinking

Write a Word Summary:

_____

_____

_____

_____

Main Idea:

Check the box that best describes all your images—the main idea.

☐ The camel can live for long periods of time in the desert when given time to rest and eat.

☐ The camel has two humps on his back that are filled with fat and that shrink when he is starving.

☐ The camel can survive in the desert without food or water due to the humps on his back that store fat for energy.

HOT Questions:

1. How do you think the camel survives for long periods of time in the hot, dry desert? _____

2. Why might the camel not have food and water in the desert? _____

3. Why do you think the camel has humps on his back? _____

4. Why do you think the humps might droop? _____

5. Why do you think a camel's humps may shrink? _____

6. Do you think the camel's humps are important? Why or why not? _____

11 Ben Franklin

Ben Franklin, one of the great men who fought for and built the United States into a country, was born in 1706. He was the 15th of 17 children of a soap and candle maker. His parents could only afford to send Ben to school for two years. So he taught himself all that he would have learned in school and more. He did this by reading every book he could while cutting wicks and melting tallow in his father's shop. He taught himself math, science, and history. He learned five languages! When he was 12, he went to work for his older brother, James, in a printing shop. There he secretly wrote news stories and James printed them. But Ben was caught and they argued. Ben left his hometown Boston at 17 to open his own print shop.

Vocabulary to Visualize:

Ben Franklin: a writer and statesman, one of the Founding Fathers who created the United States government
wicks: thread or fabric used to draw wax up to be burned in candles
tallow: the fatty parts of animals, melted and used in soap and candles
Boston: the capital city of the state of Massachusetts

1 What did those words make you picture? _____

What did you picture for...

1. Ben as a boy? _____

2. Ben teaching himself? _____

3. the candle shop? _____

4. Ben working in the print shop? _____

5. Ben as a builder of the country? _____

Critical Thinking

Write a Word Summary:

_____
_____
_____
_____
_____

Main Idea:

Check the box that best describes all your images—the main idea.

☐ Ben Franklin went to school for years learning to write news stories before he opened his own print shop in Boston, the city where he'd been born.

☐ Ben Franklin read every book he could find, and taught himself math, science, history, and five languages.

☐ Ben Franklin, who helped build the United States, taught himself everything he could, and worked in both a candle shop and a printing press.

HOT Questions:

1. Why do you think Ben couldn't stay in school? _____
_____

2. Why do you think Ben read so much? _____
_____

3. Why do you think Ben worked in the candle shop? _____
_____

4. Do you think Ben liked the candle shop job more than the print shop job? Why or why not? _____
_____

5. Why do you think Ben wrote news stories secretly? _____
_____

6. How might Ben's teaching himself might be important in creating a country? _____
_____

12 The Phoenix Rises

The phoenix was a mythical bird with bright red, gold, and purple feathers from the hot desert of Arabia. Every morning the bird would sing sweet songs to the Sun God, who rose into the sky each day. A single phoenix lived for five hundred years. Before he died, he built a raging funeral pyre and, singing, dove into it. When the flames burned out, the embers lay smoldering on the ground for a few minutes. Suddenly, a new phoenix emerged from the warm black ashes. Then the young bird flew to the palace of the honored Sun God to tell of his rebirth from the ashes.

Whole Paragraph
Date: _____

Vocabulary to Visualize:

mythical: imaginary or fictitious
Arabia: an area in Southwest Asia that includes several countries
funeral: a ceremony for the dead
pyre: a pile or heap for burning the dead
embers: small pieces of hot coal or wood in a fire
smoldering: burning without flames
rebirth: born again

1 What did those words make you picture? _____
_____
_____

What did you picture for...

1. the phoenix? _____
_____

2. the sound of his singing? _____
_____

3. the sun god? _____
_____

4. the funeral pyre? _____
_____

5. the phoenix being reborn? _____
_____

Critical Thinking

Write a Word Summary:

Main Idea:

Check the box that best describes all your images— the main idea.

☐ After five hundred years, the colorful phoenix built a raging funeral pyre before his death and dove into it, singing.

☐ The phoenix was a mythical bird that sang every morning to the Sun God as he rose up into the sky.

☐ The mythical phoenix lived for five hundred years and then dove into a fire, only to be born again in the ashes.

HOT Questions:

1. Do you think the phoenix was real? Why or why not?

2. Why do you think the phoenix sang to the Sun God?

3. Why do you think the phoenix built the funeral pyre?

4. Do you think the phoenix wanted to go into the fire?

5. Do you think the phoenix that came out of the ashes was the same one? Explain.

6. Why do you think the new phoenix went to the palace of the Sun God?

13 The Great White

The great white shark roams over a vast area of the ocean, but stays out of icy polar or hot tropical waters. His body is streamlined and bullet-shaped so he uses as little energy as possible to glide through the water. He doesn't tire out and can swim for miles. A hunter, he must keep swimming all the time to find his food. His favorite prey, seals, sea lions, and tuna, also range over a big area. To find food in the big dark oceans, he hunts by smell, sight, the taste of the water, and by feeling tiny electrical pulses given off by living things that increase as he nears them. Then he uses his powerful tail to overtake his prey.

Vocabulary to Visualize:

great white shark: a big meat-eating fish
polar: very cold; of or from the North or South Pole
tropical: very warm; near the equator
streamlined: long and rounded; slick
range: the region or space that a species lives within
pulses: a series of rhythmic movements

1 What did those words make you picture? _____

What did you picture for...

1. the great white shark? _____

2. the shark swimming? _____

3. his body as bullet-shaped? _____

4. him hunting for food? _____

5. him overtaking his prey? _____

Critical Thinking

Write a Word Summary:

_____

_____

_____

_____

_____

Main Idea:

Check the box that best describes all your images—the main idea.

☐ The great white shark tracks its prey by sight, smell, the taste of the water, and electrical pulses.

☐ The great white shark, a well-built hunter, roams over a vast area of ocean looking for food.

☐ The great white shark uses taste, smell, and sight to hunt for turtles and whales.

HOT Questions:

1. Why might the shark avoid polar waters? _____

2. Why might it be important for him to be streamlined? _____

3. Why do you think the shark has to hunt over a large area? _____

4. Why do you think the shark has so many ways to find its prey? _____

5. Why do you think the electrical pulses of his prey increase as the shark nears? _____

6. Why might it be good for the shark to have a powerful tail? _____

14 The Rose Parade

On New Year's Day, thousands of people squeeze onto the sidewalks of a street in Pasadena to watch the annual Rose Parade. The two-hour parade features bright floral floats, lively marching bands, and horseback riders. A float takes nearly a year to build and decorate. A huge frame is first built and then covered in chicken wire. A few days before the parade, flowers of all colors, types and sizes are placed all over the float to cover it entirely. The finished floats will slowly roll down the street in a line and awe the crowds with their beauty.

Vocabulary to Visualize:

New Year's Day: the first day of the calendar year, usually a holiday
Pasadena: a city in Southern California
annual: happening yearly
floats: a vehicle with a display built on it
marching band: a group of musicians
chicken wire: a light wire net, often used as a fence
awe: leave one amazed

1 What did those words make you picture? _____

What did you picture for...

1. thousands of people on the sidewalks? _____

2. the Rose Parade? _____

3. the undecorated float? _____

4. the flowers? _____

5. the finished float? _____

Critical Thinking

Write a Word Summary:

_____

_____

_____

_____

Main Idea:

Check the box that best describes all your images—the main idea.

☐ The Rose Parade is an annual event that happens on a Pasadena street in front of a large crowd.

☐ The Rose Parade starts a year earlier when the floats are built and then flowers are placed onto the frames.

☐ The Rose Parade features marching bands and floral floats that took a year to make.

HOT Questions:

1. Why do you think thousands of people squeeze around the street? _____

_____

2. Why do you think the Rose Parade only happens once a year? _____

_____

3. Why do you think the floats are covered with chicken wire? _____

_____

4. Why do you think flowers of all different colors, types and sizes are used? _____

_____

5. Why do you think it is important for the floats to travel slowly down the street? _____

_____

6. Why do you think this parade is called the "Rose Parade"? _____

_____

15 Montreal Biodome

The huge Montreal Biodome has a clear glass roof and houses four complete ecosystems. The humid tropical rainforest section has a canopy of trees that is home to monkeys, parrots, and snakes. The temperate forest has maple and fir trees and a cool stream where beavers build dams. The polar world is home to penguins that slide down the ice into a pool of frigid water. The marine world has a huge glass aquarium filled with sea life like fish and crabs. A pathway weaves through the dome and guests walk easily from one type of habitat to the next.

Whole Paragraph
Date: _____

Vocabulary to Visualize:

Montreal: a city in Quebec, part of Canada
ecosystems: a system of plants and animals interacting with their habitat
humid: hot and muggy
temperate: weather that is not too cold or too hot
polar: of or from the North or South Pole
frigid: freezing
marine: having to do with the sea
aquarium: a tank for holding fish and other live animals and plants in
habitat: living area of an animal or plant

1 What did those words make you picture? _____

What did you picture for...

1. the Montreal Biodome? _____

2. the tropical rainforest? _____

3. the temperate forest? _____

4. the polar world? _____

5. the marine world? _____

Critical Thinking

Write a Word Summary:

_____

_____

_____

_____

Main Idea:

Check the box that best describes all your images—the main idea.

☐ The Montreal Biodome houses four separate ecosystems under one roof that people can walk through.

☐ The Montreal Biodome has a tropical rainforest, a frigid polar world, and a marine world under its roof.

☐ The Montreal Biodome has a path that winds through all four ecosystems for visitors to walk on.

HOT Questions:

1. Why do you think people come to visit the Montreal Biodome? _____

_____

2. Why do you think it might be odd to have four different ecosystems all under one roof? _____

_____

3. Why do you think there are animals in the Biodome? _____

_____

4. Do you think the animals can wander from ecosystem to ecosystem? Explain. _____

_____

5. Why do you think the marine world is in an aquarium? _____

_____

6. How do you think the Biodome could help people study nature? _____

_____

16 Peary and Henson

Robert Peary and Matthew Henson were the first men to reach the North Pole in 1909. They set out from their base camp with a team of twenty-two other men, nineteen heavy sleds packed with supplies, and 133 dogs to haul them. They faced bitter cold, fierce storms, and wide canals, called leads, in the packs of ice they were walking on. When the team ran into a lead, they had to wait for it to freeze over so they could cross it. In groups of two and three, men turned back to base camp while Peary and Henson trudged on through the vast white wasteland. Finally, the two men reached the North Pole where they studied the ice and took pictures before making the journey back to base camp.

Whole Paragraph
Date: _____

Vocabulary to Visualize:

North Pole: the northernmost point on Earth
sleds: a wagon or cart that slides on runners over snow and ice
bitter: hurtful, unpleasant
fierce: violent
canals: waterways
trudged: walk with hardship; move wearily

1 What did those words make you picture? _____

_____

_____

What did you picture for...

1. the North Pole? _____

_____

2. their team of men, sleds, and dogs? _____

_____

3. the leads? _____

_____

4. trudging across the ice? _____

_____

5. them reaching the North Pole? _____

_____

Critical Thinking

Write a Word Summary:

_____

_____

_____

_____

Main Idea:

Check the box that best describes all your images—the main idea.

☐ Robert Peary and Matthew Henson were the first men to reach the North Pole after surviving bitter cold and storms.

☐ In 1909, a group of twenty-four men, 133 dogs, and nineteen heavy sleds set out from their base camp to find the North Pole.

☐ Robert Peary and Matthew Henson led a large group from their base camp to the North Pole.

HOT Questions:

1. Why do you think Peary and Henson wanted to travel to the North Pole? _____

_____

2. Why do you think they took sleds on the journey? _____

_____

3. Why do you think they took dogs on the journey? _____

_____

4. Why do you think the team had to wait for the leads to freeze? _____

_____

5. Do you think making a journey to the North Pole is dangerous? Explain. _____

_____

6. Why do you think groups of two and three men turned back but not Peary or Henson? _____

_____

17 Atlantis

Atlantis, a legendary ancient island nation, is said to have sunk in the Mediterranean Sea. It once was a glorious land of peaks, streams, rivers, and fertile soil. Near the center of the land was a large temple built on top of a high hill. Rings of canals protected the hill temple. The rulers of the nation would gather in the temple to pay tribute to their gods and talk about the laws of the land.

On a plain just next to the temple was the magnificent capital city where most of the people dwelled. The people of Atlantis were very wealthy. With its high yield of crops, the island was the center for trade with nearby lands. To help make trade easy, a long canal was carved into the land that led from the beautiful capital city to the sea. Legend has it that Atlantis was destroyed by their gods because the people became too full of pride.

Vocabulary to Visualize:

Atlantis: a legendary kingdom
Mediterranean Sea: a sea ringed by Europe, Asia, and Africa
glorious: amazing, awe-inspiring
peaks: mountains
canals: waterways
capital: the seat of government
dwelled: lived
yield: quantity or amount

---

1 **First Paragraph:** Atlantis, a legendary ancient island nation, is said to have sunk in the Mediterranean Sea. It once was a glorious land of peaks, streams, rivers, and fertile soil. Near the center of the land was a large temple built on top of a high hill. Rings of canals protected the hill temple. The rulers of the nation would gather in the temple to pay tribute to their gods and talk about the laws of the land.

What did those words make you picture? _____

What did you picture for...

1. Atlantis? _____

2. the temple? _____

3. the rings of canals? _____

4. the rulers paying tribute? _____

Paragraph by Paragraph
Date: _____

2 **Second Paragraph:** On a plain just next to the temple was the magnificent capital city where most of the people dwelled. The people of Atlantis were very wealthy. With its high yield of crops, the island was the center for trade with nearby lands. To help make trade easy, a long canal was carved into the land that led from the beautiful capital city to the sea. Legend has it that Atlantis was destroyed by their gods because the people became too full of pride.

What did those words make you picture? _____

_____

_____

What did you picture for...

1. the capital city? _____

_____

2. the crops? _____

_____

3. the long canal? _____

_____

4. the gods destroying Atlantis? _____

_____

Picture Summary:

Number your images in order.

☐ Atlantis was a glorious island nation with peaks, rivers, and streams.

☐ Atlantis was believed to have been destroyed by their gods because its people were too conceited.

☐ Atlantis had a temple on a hill, protected by canals, where the rulers met to pay tribute.

☐ A long canal was carved to help the people of Atlantis trade with nearby lands.

Write a Word Summary:

_____

_____

_____

_____

_____

_____

_____

Critical Thinking

Main Idea:

Check the box that best describes all your images—the main idea.

☐ Atlantis was a rich and powerful island nation with a temple on a hill that was surrounded by canals for protection.

☐ Atlantis was a beautiful and wealthy nation with a busy capital city that was a center for trade.

☐ Atlantis was a legendary island nation of great wealth that was submerged into the sea by the gods.

HOT Questions:

1. Why do you think the story referred to Atlantis as "legendary"? _____

2. Why do you think the temple was built on top of a hill? _____

3. Why do you think the rulers gathered in the temple? _____

4. Why do you think the people of Atlantis were so wealthy? _____

5. Why do you think Atlantis was the center for trade? _____

6. Why do you think the gods are said to have destroyed Atlantis? _____

7. Do you think Atlantis really existed? Why or why not? _____

Write a Story

Make up a story about finding the lost city of Atlantis while diving in the ocean.

_____
_____
_____
_____
_____
_____
_____
_____
_____
_____
_____
_____
_____
_____
_____
_____
_____
_____

Did you use all of the Structure Words? Check each one you used.

☐ What	☐ Number	☐ Color	☐ Mood	☐ Background	☐ Perspective
☐ Size	☐ Shape	☐ Movement	☐ Where	☐ When	☐ Sound

18 Mother Croc

The dark green crocodile is lying still on the hot sandy shore guarding her buried eggs, waiting for them to hatch. Some time later, she hears soft grunting noises coming from the eggs under the sand. She uses her big webbed feet and strong claws to dig until she sees the small white eggs. She picks up an egg between her sharp teeth and very gently bites down to crack it. A baby crocodile crawls out and falls to the soft ground.

Some of the baby crocodiles do not wait for their mother's help to hatch. They use their long snouts to break their shells and squeeze through the opening. Once all the eggs have hatched, the mother carefully picks up her babies with her long teeth and helps them into her mouth. With her mouth full, she turns and walks to the nearby swamp. She swims to a safe place and then releases her babies into their new water home.

Paragraph by Paragraph
Date: _____

Vocabulary to Visualize:

crocodile: a long thin reptile with hard skin and sharp teeth in a long jaw
guarding: protecting
webbed: having the fingers or toes connected by skin
snouts: the part of an animal's head that contains the nose and mouth
releases: lets go; sets free

---

1 **First Paragraph:** The dark green crocodile is lying still on the hot sandy shore guarding her buried eggs, waiting for them to hatch. Some time later, she hears soft grunting noises coming from the eggs under the sand. She uses her big webbed feet and strong claws to dig until she sees the small white eggs. She picks up an egg between her sharp teeth and very gently bites down to crack it. A baby crocodile crawls out and falls to the soft ground.

What did those words make you picture? _____

_____

What did you picture for...

1. the crocodile? _____

2. the grunting sounds? _____

3. her digging? _____

4. the baby crocodile crawling out? _____

2 **Second Paragraph:** Some of the baby crocodiles do not wait for their mother's help to hatch. They use their long snouts to break their shells and squeeze through the opening. Once all the eggs have hatched, the mother carefully picks up her babies with her long teeth and helps them into her mouth. With her mouth full, she turns and walks to the nearby swamp. She swims to a safe place and then releases her babies into their new water home.

What did those words make you picture? _____

_____

What did you picture for...

1. a baby crocodile trying to hatch? _____

2. the mother picking up her babies? _____

3. the mother carrying the babies? _____

4. the babies being released? _____

Picture Summary:

Number these in order.

☐ The mother crocodile releases all her babies into their wet swampy home.

☐ The crocodile mother digs gently in the sand to expose her white eggs.

☐ The crocodile mother helps some of the babies to hatch by breaking their eggs with her teeth.

☐ The mother crocodile carries her babies in her long mouth from the nest to a safe place.

Write a Word Summary:

_____

_____

_____

_____

_____

_____

Critical Thinking

Main Idea:

Check the box that best describes all your images—the main idea.

☐ The crocodile mother rests on the sand waiting for the eggs to hatch and her babies to come out of the sea.

☐ The crocodile mother protects her nest and then helps her babies to hatch before bringing them in her mouth to a safe place.

☐ The crocodile mother picks up each baby crocodile with her teeth and helps it into her mouth very gently.

HOT Questions:

1. Why do you think the crocodile needed to guard her eggs? _____

2. Why do you think the eggs were buried in the sand? _____

3. Do you think it was important that the crocodile heard the grunting noises? Why or why not? _____

4. Why do you think the crocodile cracked the eggs in her mouth? _____

5. Why do you think some of the babies didn't wait for their mother to help? _____

6. How do you think the mother was able to pick up her babies with her teeth without hurting them? _____

7. Why do you think the mother helped her babies get to the swamp water? _____

Write a Story

Make up a story about the struggle of a baby crocodile hatching.

Did you use all of the Structure Words? Check each one you used.
- ☐ What
- ☐ Size
- ☐ Number
- ☐ Shape
- ☐ Color
- ☐ Movement
- ☐ Mood
- ☐ Where
- ☐ Background
- ☐ When
- ☐ Perspective
- ☐ Sound

19 Charles Schultz

Charles Schultz created the popular comic strip, *Peanuts*. He was a smart boy who skipped two grades. In high school, he was the youngest and smallest in his class. Shy and lonely, he spent all his time reading newspaper comics, and drawing each one over and over again. When other kids saw his work, they surprised the artist by asking him to draw for them.

After high school, Charles worked on his own comic strip. *Peanuts* was about a group of kids. One was Charlie Brown, a short, clumsy, and shy boy. Like other boys, he had a crush on the little red-haired girl in his class. He was nervous and he made mistakes, just like real kids do.

Charles could not believe how popular his comic strip became. People wrote him letters praising his simple drawings and funny jokes. These people had trouble talking with strangers and winning baseball games when they were young, just like Charlie Brown and his friends.

Vocabulary to Visualize:

popular: admired by a group of people; well liked

comic strip: a picture story, usually funny or adventurous

newspaper: a printed paper containing daily or weekly information

---

1 **First Paragraph:** Charles Schultz created the popular comic strip, *Peanuts*. He was a smart boy who skipped two grades. In high school, he was the youngest and smallest in his class. Shy and lonely, he spent all his time reading newspaper comics, and drawing each one over and over again. When other kids saw his work, they surprised the artist by asking him to draw for them.

What did those words make you picture? _____

_____

What did you picture for...

1. Charles Schultz as a boy? _____

2. skipping two grades? _____

3. Charles reading newspaper comics? _____

4. Charles drawing? _____

2 **Second Paragraph:** After high school, Charles worked on his own comic strip. *Peanuts* was about a group of kids. One was Charlie Brown, a short, clumsy, and shy boy. Like other boys, he had a crush on the little red-haired girl in his class. He was nervous and he made mistakes, just like real kids do.

What did those words make you picture? _____

_____

_____

What did you picture for...

1. Charlie Brown? _____

   _____

2. him having a crush on the girl? _____

   _____

3. him making mistakes? _____

   _____

3 **Third Paragraph:** Charles could not believe how popular his comic strip became. People wrote him letters praising his simple drawings and funny jokes. These people had trouble talking with strangers and winning baseball games when they were young, just like Charlie Brown and his friends.

What did those words make you picture? _____

_____

What did you picture for...

1. Charles' strip being popular? _____

   _____

2. people writing him letters? _____

   _____

3. his simple drawings? _____

   _____

4. the readers as kids? _____

   _____

Critical Thinking

Picture Summary:

Number your images in order.

☐ Charles Schultz drew his own comic strip, which was about kids like him that had funny, real problems.

☐ Charles Schultz was a lonely and shy boy two grades ahead in school, but other kids liked his artwork.

☐ Charles Schultz created characters like Charlie Brown, a kid like he was, and his comic strip *Peanuts* became very popular.

Main Idea:

Check the box that best describes all your images—the main idea.

☐ Charles Schultz was shy and lonely in high school, so he spent all his time drawing and reading newspapers.

☐ Charles Schultz was a small and clumsy child, and skipped two grades to be the youngest kid in the high school, which made him shy.

☐ Charles Schultz made a comic strip called Peanuts full of funny kids making mistakes like real kids, and people loved it.

HOT Questions:

1. Why do you think Charles was able to skip two grades? _____

2. Why might it have been hard for Charles to make friends in high school? _____

3. Why might Charles have decided to create a comic strip? _____

4. Where do you think Charles got the idea for Charlie Brown? Why? _____

5. Why do you think Charles made his characters funny? _____

6. Where do you think he got the ideas for the other characters in his comic strip? _____

Write a Story

Make up a story about anything you want!

_____
_____
_____
_____
_____
_____
_____
_____
_____
_____
_____
_____
_____
_____
_____
_____
_____

Did you use all of the Structure Words? Check each one you used.
- ☐ What
- ☐ Size
- ☐ Number
- ☐ Shape
- ☐ Color
- ☐ Movement
- ☐ Mood
- ☐ Where
- ☐ Background
- ☐ When
- ☐ Perspective
- ☐ Sound

20 Preparing for Winter

Paragraph by Paragraph
Date: _____

The Aleuts are a native tribe that survives in a harsh land. They live on islands off the coast of icy Alaska. Many Aleut men still hunt and fish for the tribe's food. The women sew clothes, weave baskets and mats, and cook hearty meals.

When the weather becomes warmer, the men leave their arctic villages to set up fishing camps. They fill their sturdy wooden boats with food, animal furs, and fresh water. After paddling to warmer waters, they set up a row of tents along the shore. The next two months they catch enough food to last the tribe through the winter. Their ivory fishhooks and long spears help them catch plenty of fish.

Back at home, the women are busy preparing for the winter weather. They patch up any holes in their sunken homes with dry grass. They add whalebones to support the roof. Then they lay out extra animal skins on their beds. The village will be ready when the men return. Then they'll all hunker down for the icy winter months.

Vocabulary to Visualize:

Aleuts: the people who live on the Aleutian Islands
harsh: severe, uncomfortable; rugged
Alaska: a state in the U.S.
arctic: of or from the north pole
ivory: substance from the tusks of elephants and walruses
hunker: to take shelter; to hide out

---

1 **First Paragraph:** The Aleuts are a native tribe that survives in a harsh land. They live on islands off the coast of icy Alaska. Many Aleut men still hunt and fish for the tribe's food. The women sew clothes, weave baskets and mats, and cook hearty meals.

What did those words make you picture? _____

_____

What did you picture for...

1. the Aleuts surviving in a harsh land? _____

2. islands in Alaska? _____

3. the men hunting and fishing? _____

4. the women weaving and cooking? _____

2 **Second Paragraph:** When the weather becomes warmer, the men leave their arctic villages to set up fishing camps. They fill their sturdy wooden boats with food, animal furs, and fresh water. After paddling to warmer waters, they set up a row of tents along the shore. The next two months they catch enough food to last the tribe through the winter. Their ivory fishhooks and long spears help them catch plenty of fish.

What did those words make you picture? _____

_____

What did you picture for...

1. the men leaving in warm weather? _____

_____

2. filling the boats and paddling? _____

_____

3. the fishing camp? _____

_____

4. the ivory fishhooks? _____

_____

3 **Third Paragraph:** Back at home, the women are busy preparing for the winter weather. They patch up any holes in their sunken homes with dry grass. They add whalebones to support the roof. Then they lay out extra animal skins on their beds. The village will be ready when the men return. Then they'll all hunker down for the icy winter months.

What did those words make you picture? _____

_____

What did you picture for...

1. the women patching holes? _____

_____

2. the whalebones? _____

_____

3. their beds? _____

_____

4. the Aleuts hunkering down? _____

_____

Critical Thinking

Picture Summary:

Number your images in order.

☐ The Aleut men set up fishing camps and catch enough fish for the whole tribe for winter.

☐ The Aleut tribe lives on islands in Alaska, where many hunt and fish for food.

☐ The Aleut women repair the roofs of the houses and make the camp ready for the icy winter.

Main Idea:

Check the box that best describes all your images—the main idea.

☐ The Aleut men pack their wood boats with food, water, and furs and prepare for the winter by fishing with ivory fishhooks and spears.

☐ The Aleut tribe hunts and fishes for food on the islands of Alaska, where they live for only a few months of the year to prepare for winter.

☐ The Aleut tribe gets ready for winter by having men fish for food and women prepare the homes.

HOT Questions:

1. Why do you think the Aleuts have to work so hard to get ready for the winter months? _____

2. Why do the men leave their arctic villages when it starts to get warm? _____

3. Why do the men have to catch so much food? _____

4. Why do the women patch holes and support the roof with more whalebones? _____

5. Why do they have to put more animal skins on the beds? _____

6. Why do you think the Aleuts hunker down for winter? Do you think they go out much? Why or why not? _____

Write a Story

Make up a story about an Aleut village preparing for winter.

Did you use all of the Structure Words? Check each one you used.
- ☐ What
- ☐ Number
- ☐ Color
- ☐ Mood
- ☐ Background
- ☐ Perspective
- ☐ Size
- ☐ Shape
- ☐ Movement
- ☐ Where
- ☐ When
- ☐ Sound

21 Cage Diving with Sharks

The dangerous great white shark can be safely viewed and photographed from inside an underwater metal cage. Minced fish bait, called chum, is dumped into the water to attract a shark to a drifting boat. Then rope is tied onto the tails of whole fish and they are dangled in the water as bait.

A huge great white shark senses the food from far away and uses her strong fins to swim to it. Once the shark is spotted near the boat, a diver slides into the hole at the top of the steel cage floating in the ocean. His thick wetsuit keeps him warm while in the cold water. He puts in his mouthpiece, allowing him to breathe while he is underwater. Then the top of the cage is closed.

The cage is lowered into the water a few feet. The diver gazes out at the deadly shark only inches away. The diver observes the shark as he takes pictures of it gliding in the water and feeding on the bait with her razor sharp teeth.

Vocabulary to Visualize:

great white shark: a big meat-eating fish
minced: chopped into small pieces
attract: bring towards; draw to
diver: a person who dives into deep water using a breathing device
wetsuit: a close-fitting rubber garment worn by a diver to insulate the body against cold
observes: watches or sees
razor: sharp edged; cutting

1 **First Paragraph:** The dangererous great white shark can be safely viewed and photographed from inside an underwater metal cage. Minced fish bait, called chum, is dumped into the water to attract a shark to a drifting boat. Then rope is tied onto the tails of whole fish and they are dangled in the water as bait.

What did those words make you picture? _____

_____

What did you picture for...

1. the great white shark? _____

2. the underwater cage? _____

3. chum? _____

4. the boat? _____

2 **Second Paragraph:** A huge great white shark senses the food from far away and uses her strong fins to swim to it. Once the shark is spotted near the boat, a diver slides into the hole at the top of the steel cage floating in the ocean. His thick wetsuit keeps him warm while in the cold water. He puts in his mouthpiece, allowing him to breathe while he is underwater. Then the top of the cage is closed.

What did those words make you picture? _____

_____

What did you picture for...

1. the diver getting into the cage? _____

   _____

2. the shark sensing the food? _____

   _____

3. the diver's wetsuit? _____

   _____

4. the mouthpiece? _____

   _____

3 **Third Paragraph:** The cage is lowered into the water a few feet. The diver gazes out at the deadly shark only inches away. The diver observes the shark as he takes pictures of it gliding in the water and feeding on the bait with her razor sharp teeth.

What did those words make you picture? _____

_____

What did you picture for...

1. the cage being lowered? _____

   _____

2. the diver taking pictures? _____

   _____

3. the shark in the water? _____

   _____

4. the shark feeding? _____

   _____

Critical Thinking

Picture Summary:

Number your images in order.

☐ The diver gets in the cage and is lowered into the water.

☐ The shark feeds just inches from the diver as he photographs her.

☐ Chum is used to attract the shark to the drifting boat.

Main Idea:

Check the box that best describes all your images—the main idea.

☐ A metal cage protects the diver as he photographs a great white shark feeding in the ocean.

☐ The great white shark can sense the food in the water and swims over to the boat to feed with razor-sharp teeth.

☐ The boat drifts in the ocean and chum is thrown into the water to attract a great white shark near enough to be caged.

HOT Questions:

1. Do you think the great white shark is dangerous? Why or why not? _____

2. Why do you think minced fish was dumped in the water? _____

3. Why do you think the chum might attract a shark? _____

4. Do you think it is important for the diver to be in a cage while taking pictures? Why or why not? _____

5. Why do you think the cage is lowered into the water? _____

6. Why do you think the diver takes pictures of the shark? _____

Write a Story

Make up a story about a diver swimming with sharks with no cage.

___

Did you use all of the Structure Words? Check each one you used.
- ☐ What
- ☐ Size
- ☐ Number
- ☐ Shape
- ☐ Color
- ☐ Movement
- ☐ Mood
- ☐ Where
- ☐ Background
- ☐ When
- ☐ Perspective
- ☐ Sound

22 Life in the Outback

The dark-skinned aborigines that first dwelled in Australia were able to adapt to the very dry country. They lived in groups called clans, moving from place to place to look for food and water. Water could not always be found above the ground when the rivers dried up. But the clans knew where underground rivers flowed and dug wells to them. They kept the water in kangaroo skin bags and baskets made from palm leaves.

The men and women both hunted for food. They also ate roots, fruits, and berries. The men fished in the sea using spears and nets, catching sea turtles and sharks. Fire was used for cooking the food, making tools, and keeping people warm. They also used fire when hunting to lead their prey to where it could be easily caught.

Paragraph by Paragraph
Date:_____

Vocabulary to Visualize:

outback: the dry, harsh lands in Australia
aborigines: the native people of Australia
Australia: an island continent between the Indian and Pacific oceans
wells: holes in the ground dug to get to underground fluid
kangaroo: a large animal with big hind legs used for jumping, and a large tail
prey: an animal hunted for food

---

1 **First Paragraph:** The dark-skinned aborigines that first dwelled in Australia were able to adapt to the very dry country. They lived in groups called clans, moving from place to place to look for food and water. Water could not always be found above the ground when the rivers dried up. But the clans knew where underground rivers flowed and dug wells to them. They kept the water in kangaroo skins bags and baskets made from palm leaves.

What did those words make you picture?_____

_____

What did you picture for...

1. the aborigines living in the dry country? _____

2. the clans? _____

3. them digging wells? _____

4. the bags and baskets they kept water in? _____

2 **Second Paragraph:** The men and women both hunted for food. They also ate roots, fruits, and berries. The men fished in the sea using spears and nets, catching sea turtles and sharks. Fire was used for cooking the food, making tools, and keeping people warm. They also used fire when hunting to lead their prey to where it could be easily caught.

What did those words make you picture? _____

_____

What did you picture for...

1. the men and women hunting for food? _____

2. roots, fruits, and berries? _____

3. the men fishing? _____

4. them using fire to hunt? _____

Picture Summary:

Number your images in order.

- The aborigines lived in the very dry country of Australia in groups called clans.

- The aborigines dug wells to reach the underground rivers and stored the water in skin bags and baskets.

- The aborigines hunted, fished, and collected food from the land and sea.

- The aborigines used fire for warmth, cooking, and hunting.

Write a Word Summary:

_____
_____
_____
_____
_____
_____
_____

Critical Thinking

Main Idea:

Check the box that best describes all your images—the main idea.

☐ The aborigines of Australia have learned to survive in the outback.

☐ The aborigines hunted, fished, and gathered food from the wet country around them.

☐ The aborigines move from place to place around Australia looking for water.

HOT Questions:

1. How do you think the aborigines were able to adapt to the very dry country? _____

2. Why do you think they lived in groups? _____

3. Why do you think they moved from place to place? _____

4. Why do you think they used kangaroo skin bags to collect water and not a bucket? _____

5. Do you think it was important for them to know where underground rivers flowed? Why or why not? _____

6. Why do you think they dug wells? _____

7. How do you think fire helped lead prey? _____

Write a Story

Make up an adventure story about an aborigine hunt.

Did you use all of the Structure Words? Check each one you used.
- ☐ What
- ☐ Number
- ☐ Color
- ☐ Mood
- ☐ Background
- ☐ Perspective
- ☐ Size
- ☐ Shape
- ☐ Movement
- ☐ Where
- ☐ When
- ☐ Sound

23 Bruce Lee

Bruce Lee was a famous martial artist who created his own style of fighting. He was born in San Francisco but moved to Hong Kong as a child. He grew up learning Asian martial arts. He returned to the U.S. at eighteen and taught martial arts. He invented the famous "One-Inch Punch." Lee would stand with one arm extended and punch, barely moving his arm, and could knock a man off his feet.

He opened an institute where he taught martial arts to non-Asians. This was not very common at the time and he was challenged to a fight over it. If Lee lost the fight, he would close his school. Lee used his skill to win but was frustrated that the fight took so long. He decided to change his style.

He studied a variety of martial arts. He found them stiff, not practical for real fighting. He mixed the best of each martial art into his own style, called Jeet Kune Do. Lee later showed his fast fighting in martial art films.

Vocabulary to Visualize:

martial artist: a person skilled in forms of combat or defense
San Francisco: a city in California, one of the states of the U.S.
Hong Kong: a large city in China
Asian: of or from to Asia
extended: stretched out
institute: school or training center

1 **First Paragraph:** Bruce Lee was a famous martial artist who created his own style of fighting. He was born in San Francisco but moved to Hong Kong as a child. He grew up learning Asian martial arts. He returned to the U.S. at eighteen and taught martial arts. He invented the famous "One-Inch Punch." Lee would stand with one arm extended and punch, barely moving his arm, and could knock a man off his feet.

What did those words make you picture? _____

What did you picture for...

1. Bruce Lee as a martial artist? _____

2. Lee learning martial arts? _____

3. the "One-Inch Punch"? _____

4. Lee knocking a man off his feet? _____

2 **Second Paragraph:** He opened an institute where he taught martial arts to non-Asians. This was not very common at the time and he was challenged to a fight over it. If Lee lost the fight, he would close his school. Lee used his skill to win but was frustrated that the fight took so long. He decided to change his style.

   What did those words make you picture? _____

_____

What did you picture for...

1. his institute? _____

_____

2. non-Asians? _____

_____

3. him being challenged to a fight? _____

_____

4. Lee frustrated?_____

_____

3 **Third Paragraph:** He studied a variety of martial arts. He found them stiff, not practical for real fighting. He mixed the best of each martial art into his own style, called Jeet Kune Do. Lee later showed his fast fighting in martial art films.

   What did those words make you picture?_____

_____

What did you picture for...

1. Bruce studying a variety of martial arts? _____

_____

2. Bruce mixing styles? _____

_____

3. martial arts films? _____

_____

4. Bruce in martial arts films?_____

_____

Critical Thinking

Picture Summary:

Number your images in order.

- Bruce Lee combined the best of all the martial arts styles into Jeet Kune Do, his own style, and showed it off in films.

- Bruce Lee was born in the U.S., but learned martial arts while growing up in Hong Kong, where he invented the "One-Inch Punch."

- Bruce Lee returned to the U.S. and opened an institute to teach martial arts to non-Asians.

Main Idea:

Check the box that best describes all your images—the main idea.

- ☐ Bruce Lee was a famous martial artist who both taught his own style of fighting and fought in films in Hong Kong.

- ☐ Bruce Lee invented the "One-Inch Punch," in which he stood with his arm extended and barely moved it, yet knocked a man off his feet.

- ☐ Bruce Lee learned martial arts in Hong Kong and taught in the U.S. before developing his own style called Jeet Kune Do.

HOT Questions:

1. Why do you think Bruce Lee was famous? _____

2. Why do you think Bruce began to teach others martial arts? _____

3. Who might have gotten upset that Bruce was teaching martial arts to non-Asians? Why? _____

4. Why do you think Bruce studied all martial art styles? _____

5. Why do you think Lee combined the best of the martial arts for his new style? _____

6. Why do you think Lee made martial arts films? _____

Write a Story

Make up a story about Bruce Lee in a fight.

Did you use all of the Structure Words? Check each one you used.

- ☐ What
- ☐ Number
- ☐ Color
- ☐ Mood
- ☐ Background
- ☐ Perspective
- ☐ Size
- ☐ Shape
- ☐ Movement
- ☐ Where
- ☐ When
- ☐ Sound

24 Walking to the Olympics

In 300 B.C., two brothers got ready for the long journey from Athens to watch the Olympics. They had heard exciting stories about the sports games and wanted to see them. The walk would cover many miles but they were both young and strong. So they put on their best sandals, grabbed their money pouches and walking sticks, and set out for Olympia.

The brothers started out on a paved road of smooth gray stones. As the road wound into the hills, it turned to rough dirt. They passed white cliffs plunging into the blue ocean. Some of the trail crossed narrow ledges of crumbling dirt. They were both glad when they finally made it to Olympia.

The brothers were amazed at the crowd there. Only the rich could afford a hotel, so they had to sleep outside. Even when the boys found a spot shaded by a tree, the noise of the crowd kept them up all night. But at the start of the games, they forgot all about that and proudly cheered the athletes.

Vocabulary to Visualize:

Olympics: athletic games held once every four years, begun in ancient times
pouches: small bags
Athens: the capital city of Greece (in ancient times, a city-state of its own)
Olympia: a plain in Greece where the Olympics were held in ancient times
plunging: descending violently or abruptly

1 **First Paragraph:** In 300 B.C., two brothers got ready for the long journey from Athens to watch the Olympics. They had heard exciting stories about the sports games and wanted to see them. The walk would cover many miles but they were both young and strong. So they put on their best sandals, grabbed their money pouches and walking sticks, and set out for Olympia.
What did those words make you picture? _____

What did you picture for...

1. the brothers? _____

2. the journey? _____

3. Athens in 300 B.C.? _____

4. their money pouches? _____

2 **Second Paragraph:** The brothers started out on a paved road of smooth gray stones. As the road wound into the hills, it turned to rough dirt. They passed white cliffs plunging into the blue ocean. Some of the trail crossed narrow ledges of crumbling dirt. They were both glad when they finally made it to Olympia.
   What did those words make you picture? _____

_____

What did you picture for...

1. the brothers starting out? _____

_____

2. the rough dirt road? _____

_____

3. the white cliffs? _____

_____

4. the trail? _____

_____

3 **Third Paragraph:** The brothers were amazed at the crowd there. Only the rich could afford a hotel, so they had to sleep outside. Even when the boys found a spot shaded by a tree, the noise of the crowd kept them up all night. But at the start of the games, they forgot all about that and proudly cheered the athletes.
   What did those words make you picture? _____

_____

What did you picture for...

1. the crowd? _____

_____

2. where the brothers slept? _____

_____

3. the sound of the crowd? _____

_____

4. the start of the games? _____

_____

Critical Thinking

Picture Summary:

Number your images in order.

- The brothers had to walk on crumbling ledges along cliffs that plunged to the sea below before reaching Olympia.

- The brothers got ready and set out from Athens to walk the many miles to the Olympics.

- The brothers found a spot in Olympia to sleep but got little rest before the games began.

Main Idea:

Check the box that best describes all your images—the main idea.

- ☐ Two brothers slept under a tree in the valley of Olympia after a long journey over paved roads, dirt, and crumbling ledges.

- ☐ Two brothers got ready to set off on a journey by getting their money pouches, putting on sandals, and picking up their walking sticks.

- ☐ Two brothers made the sometimes dangerous journey from Athens to Olympia to watch the athletic games of the Olympics.

HOT Questions:

1. Why do you think the brothers wanted to go to the Olympics? _____

2. Why might they have had to walk to Olympia? _____

3. Do you think the walk was dangerous? Why or why not? _____

4. Do you think the Olympics were popular in Greece? Why or why not? _____

5. Why do you think the brothers could not stay at the hotel? _____

6. Where do you think the games got their name from? _____

Write a Story

Make up a story about something that the brothers saw on their journey.

_____
_____
_____
_____
_____
_____
_____
_____
_____
_____
_____
_____
_____
_____
_____
_____
_____
_____
_____
_____

Did you use all of the Structure Words? Check each one you used.
- ☐ What
- ☐ Size
- ☐ Number
- ☐ Shape
- ☐ Color
- ☐ Movement
- ☐ Mood
- ☐ Where
- ☐ Background
- ☐ When
- ☐ Perspective
- ☐ Sound

Notes

Analysis of Student Performance:

_____
_____
_____
_____
_____
_____
_____
_____
_____
_____
_____
_____
_____
_____
_____

Visualizing and Verbalizing® *Graded Workbooks* **Color Coding**

The colored checkers along the book's spine represent the grade level of the workbook. For example, the six orange checkers indicate that the workbook is written at a sixth grade reading level. The colored star helps differentiate between books a, b, and c in each workbook set.